Chairman Mao Zedong

WORKERS OF THE WORLD, UNITE!

PREFACE

An Editor's Note, 1972

In recent years there occurred in China an upsurge in the mass movement to study Chairman Mao's brilliant philosophic thinking. The broad masses of workers, peasants and soldiers at the forefront of the upsurge study philosophy in the three great revolutionary movements of class struggle, the struggle for production and scientific experiment. With philosophy as their sharp weapon, they untangle the knotty problems facing them, especially the problems arising in the course of the struggle between the two lines — the proletarian revolutionary line and the counter-revolutionary revisionist line, between socialism and capitalism.

Our great leader Chairman Mao's call: "*Liberate philosophy from the confines of the philosophers' lecture rooms and textbooks, and turn it into a sharp weapon in the hands of the masses*" is becoming revolutionary reality.

Why do workers, peasants and soldiers study philosophy? How do they study and what do they gain from their study? Answers to these questions will be found in these stories from Chinchien Production Brigade in one of the people's communes in China's Chekiang Province.

The experience of Chinchien in studying philosophy proves beyond doubt that workers, peasants and soldiers can master philosophy, because they study in the struggle and for the struggle. Their study of philosophy is necessary for the three revolutionary movements and for proletarian dictatorship.

Chinchien's experience shows also that only by relating philosophic study with the problems arising in the three great revolutionary movements, especially in the course of the struggle between socialism and capitalism, can the study yield rich results.

contents

HOW DID THE STUDY OF PHILOSOPHY START?

What Were the Contradictions?

This collection of accounts from Chinchien Production Brigade of Kiangshan County, Chekiang Province, tells something of the commune members' study and application of Chairman Mao's philosophic work "*On Contradiction*".

As for contradictions, they do exist objectively, always and everywhere, and everyone has to deal with them every day. But to correctly understand the nature of contradictions, and solve them, is quite another thing.

The Chinchien Brigade is situated on the border between Chekiang and Kiangsi provinces, its more than 800 *mu* (1/6 Acre) of farmland embracing over thirteen plots of loess hilly slopes. The soil was poor, and even when it rained the water rushed down the slopes and could not be stored. Before the liberation, the poor and lower middle peasants there lived worse than animals under the heel of Kuomintang reactionaries, landlords and rich peasants. After the liberation they received their own land, but because of individual farming, some became poor for lack of labour power or for other reasons, and had to sell their land. Thus polarization arose. Then, agricultural co-operatives were set up in the Chinchien area. In 1955 the renegade, hidden traitor and scab Liu Shao-chi and his agents in Chekiang Province drastically slashed the number of co-operatives in an effort to strangle the co-operative movement.

But the poor and lower-middle peasants of the brigade frustrated Liu's scheme. Chairman Mao's timely report, "On the Question of Agricultural Co-operation", supported them. Production developed rapidly. During the three years from 1960 to 1962 when China's national economy met with temporary difficulties, Liu Shao-chi fanned up the evil wind of *san zi yi bao*,* which also blew into the brigade. The comrades once again succeeded in repelling it, but not without exerting strenuous efforts.

For many years, such cadres as the secretary and deputy secretary of the brigade Party branch Chiang Juwang and Tai Hsiang-mei, actually dealt with contradictions every day. So did the poor and lower-middle peasant rank-and-file of the brigade. Still they did not understand the nature of contradictions and attributed the difficulties and conflicts they encountered in their work to underdeveloped collective economy and the peasants' low living standard. They thought the difficulties and contradictions would disappear in the future when they were better off.

By 1963 the average grain yield of the brigade had increased from 300 *jin* (1/2 kilogram) per mu in the early years after liberation to 813 *jin*. The collective economy throve, and a number of the commune members had built new houses, while there was great over-all improvement of the peasants' livelihood. According to the above logic, the contradictions would naturally disappear. But they had not.

Prosperity caused some in the brigade to slip backwards and stop revolutionizing their thinking. The idea that "it doesn't pay to be a cadre" arose in the minds of some cadres, who did not want to shoulder responsibilities. And some people thought that "the brigade's production has reached its maximum".

---

* San zi yi bao means the extension of the free market, extension of private plots, increase of small enterprises with sole responsibility for their own profits or losses, and the fixing of output quotas on the individual households.

The comrades of the Party branch were also faced with a number of vexing problems, one of which concerned the use of fish ponds.

Every production team under the brigade has ponds, and the majority of the members held that the ponds should be used for collective fish breeding so as to strengthen the collective economy. But a few members with a spontaneous tendency towards capitalism disagreed, saying the ponds should be rented to individuals for private fish breeding. After repeated arguments the leader of a production team finally accepted the latter proposal, and it seemed that the contradiction had vanished.

During a dry spell in the summer of 1964, when the fresh green rice seedlings were beginning to turn yellow, the production team leader thought it best to irrigate the paddy fields with pond water. But a member engaged in private fish breeding said: "Does it mean my fish fry will all die, with the ponds drained?" Here was a contradiction. What was to be done?

The team leader said: "Let's discuss the matter. Shall we irrigate with pond water or not? We'll make a decision."

"Of course, we'll use the pond water. Can we let the fields dry up and bring a loss to the collective while the pond water stands idle? This is without rhyme or reason," the team members replied.

When the plan for irrigation was put into action, the fish breeder was very irritated and said: "You agreed to private fish raising at first. Now you drain the ponds for irrigation. The two decisions are contradictory."

The team leader lost his temper and retorted, "You yourselves are contradictory too!" They debated the problem for a long time but could not solve it. Then they approached Comrade Chiang Ju-wang for his view.

Several teams had the same contradiction, which became very sharp. Ju-wang and other comrades of the Party branch

Felt only that it was wrong to let members work at private fish raising in ponds that belonged to the collective, but they lacked other arguments to convince the members concerned, and the problem remained unsolved.

In the autumn of that year the "four clean-ups" movement* was launched in the Chinchien Brigade. Chiang Ju-wang and Tai Hsiang-mei greeted the movement as the solution to most of the contradictions in the brigade.

However, the movement itself was full of contradictions and struggles. At the initial stage a work team sent to the brigade followed Liu Shao-chi's bourgeois reactionary line, and checked the family-status records as soon as they entered the village, saying that a poor and lower-middle peasants' association was to be set up. This association would not admit any peasant from a poor or lower-middle peasant family who had been a cadre at any time after the liberation. Thus the cadres were indiscriminately all brushed aside. The work team trusted anyone who spoke against the cadres. The member who was engaged in private fish breeding raised his case before the work team. Taking this opportunity, some ex-landlords and rich peasants even tried to reverse the verdicts passed on them, and reactionary arrogance held sway. Instead of checking the ill wind the work team nagged at the cadres, placing itself at odds with the Party branch. Pointing to the cadres, one of the work team said: "The 'four cleans' and the 'four uncleans' form the principal contradiction of the rural areas at present. The focus of the contradiction is on you."

These words jolted the comrades of the Party branch. What was the "principal contradiction", and the "focus of contradiction"? What were their contradictions after all? How were they to handle them? They resented that work team member's remarks.

Refers to the socialist education movement to clean things up in the- fields of politics, ideology, organization and - economy.

Heated discussion followed but gave no result.

What a heap of contradictions for Ju-wang and his comrades to sort out! He recalled the departing words in 1959 of the Liberation Army men who had helped them consolidate the people's commune and rectify the style of work. The Army men's words were: "Study Chairman Mao's works and find answers from them whenever you come across problems." His mind cleared. Looking at his comrades confidently he said: "Contradictions everywhere; what kind of contradictions are they after all? Isn't there an article '*On Contradiction*' by Chairman Mao? That will certainly solve our contradictions!"

That was when the comrades of the Party branch began to study "On Contradiction".

A Tortuous Course

It was not plain sailing for the comrades of the Party branch to study and apply Chairman Mao's philosophic works. Their course was full of twists and turns.

How should they study? This was their first question. They began by reading through the article paragraph by paragraph, much as students in school might, without stressing how the specific problems at hand were to be solved. Every evening, sitting around the Party branch secretary Chiang Ju-wang, the Party members listened while he read out "*On Contradiction*". Though Chiang had only a few years of schooling, it was a little more than his comrades' average education. This was the first time he had read a philosophic essay. Many of the words were unfamiliar, and he stumbled along, while the listeners felt dizzy. What was philosophy after all? What was contradiction? They read for several evenings, but still could not understand.

Though the philosophic study had yielded no results, word of it got about and the class enemy, feeling that the Party members' study of philosophy was not in their interest, began blasting the Party cadres. "Humph! Clodhoppers wanting to study philosophy! It's as ridiculous as a cat teaching tigers to climb a tree. And these are blind tigers at that."

Some in the village with a smattering of education were influenced by the fallacy that "philosophy is mysterious" spread by Liu Shao-chi and his agent in philosophical circles Yang Hsien-chen, and also considered philosophy quite beyond the poor and lower-middle peasants 5 comprehension. At those who had the courage to study philosophy, they sneered, "Do you think you can understand what you're studying? Even when you buy a hat you have to consider your head-size!"

While the Party branch comrades studied "*On Contradiction*", the contradictions in the village kept mounting. A member of the 11th production team had sold his fish fry during the fight against the drought. Now, taking advantage of the attack on cadres by some of the work team, he demanded compensation by the production team for his loss due to selling the fry so young. The production team store-keeper could not decide the issue and asked Chiang Ju-wang 5 s opinion. Chiang said there should be no compensation. The work team said he was wrong, that he had taken a wrong stand, and that a mass meeting should be held to criticize him. The work team even tried to dismiss the 11th production team leader, and the store-keeper was actually replaced by a bad element.

The Party branch comrades were indignant at this and no longer read paragraph by paragraph but debated the incident, each voicing his views. All agreed that here was a real contradiction indeed. Why did the work team describe a crystal-clear right thing as wrong and a wrong thing as right?

Why does it trust only some persons with bad records and a serious spontaneous tendency towards capitalism?" questioned Tai Hsiang-mei.

Another joined in, "I belong to the poor and lower middle peasant class too and might have been one of those the work team relied on if not for being a cadre for a time after the liberation."

And another said: "What is that about the contradiction between the 'four cleans' and the 'four uncleans' being the principal contradiction in the countryside? Did we cadres all commit the 'four uncleans' errors? Is none of us any good?"

After that, they naturally turned from reading to discussing the practical problems, and laid the article On Contradiction" aside and failed to apply what they read to help solve their problems. The more they discussed, the more they felt something was wrong and concluded that the contradictions were complex, and so they could not get a clear picture of them. Then, the work team hurriedly withdrew on New Year's eve.

Like a clap of spring thunder, the "23-Point Document" ("Some Current Problems Raised in the Socialist Education Movement in the Rural Areas") reached the village. It had been drafted under the direction of Chairman Mao himself and greatly excited the comrades of the Party branch. They studied this important document word by word and sentence by sentence. In it Chairman Mao refuted Liu Shao-chi's fallacy of "contradiction be-tween 'four cleans' and 'four uncleans' ", and made it very clear that the present movement was to resolve the contradiction between socialism and capitalism. He also emphasized that the majority of cadres are good or relatively good, and that the main target in the present movement was those Party persons in power taking the capitalist road.

Chairman Mao's instructions enlightened the comrades of the Chinchien Brigade, and they combined their study of "On Contradiction" with that of the "23-Point Document",

And their study with their own experience. They began to realize that of the numerous contradictions the principal one is that between the proletariat and the bourgeoisie, between the socialist and the capitalist roads. What was the contradiction to be solved in the socialist education movement? It should be the contradiction between the two classes and the two roads, and not any socalled contradiction between the "four cleans" and "four uncleans" or between commune members and cadres. What about the nature of the private fish raising question? Was it a contradiction between fish raising and irrigating with pond water? In the final analysis, it was a contradiction between the two roads. Many questions, which they had been unable to explain before, became clear, once they grasped the principal contradiction.

But the Party branch comrades' first attempts at integrating theory with practice were by trial and error, and the old force of habit was strong. The old methods of book-delving crept back, and they ran into snags again. For example, though they had grasped the principal contradiction, they still did not understand many concepts, like the principal aspect of a contradiction, and others.

"Is it because we have no education?" asked someone.

"Perhaps."

"Then let's ask someone with a higher education to give us a lecture, give us some enlightenment."

Thus the Party branch invited three senior middle school students as their teachers. True, they knew more words and read more fluently than Chiang. But smooth reading was not what the Party members required. They wanted to learn to grasp Chairman Mao's revolutionary teachings. They raised the question: "What is meant by 'the principal aspect of a contradiction'?"

"The principal aspect of a contradiction, eh..." one of the students answered. He hadn't got it either, and became flustered.

"The principal aspect of a contradiction is the principal aspect of a contradiction. What's there to explain about that?"

By this time some of those in the study class lost heart and said: "Let's give up! So many difficulties in our study of philosophy. It's enough for us farmers to know how to farm."

But the old poor peasant Chiang Cheng-liang had stronger determination, and said, "We studied Chairman Mao's articles 'Serve the People', 'In Memory of Norman Bethune' and 'The Foolish Old Man Who Removed the Mountains', and got a lot out of it. Why can't we study 'On Contradiction'? It depends on the way we study it."

Others in the study class discussed the question and said: "We studied those three articles well because we applied what we studied in solving the problems that faced us. This experience is also useful in studying philosophy. We study philosophy because we have problems, but when we turned to books we put the problems aside. Therefore we should study what relates to our specific problems and apply what we study to solve them."

Chiang Ju-wang summed up the discussion thus: "Right, in studying philosophy, we should integrate it with our experience in the three great revolutionary movements of class struggle, the struggle for production and scientific experiment and with our ideological problems, and apply our study to solve them too."

A Tortuous Course

After going back and forth several times between study and application, the Party branch comrades got a better idea of what was meant by applying study to specific problems. Next was to determine what their specific problems were. They placed two questions on the table: one, the idea that "it doesn't pay to be a cadre", and the other, that "production has reached its maximum".

Animated discussion followed, Chiang Ju-wang leading off. "Taking ourselves as example, we used to say that our livelihood was not quite ideal and that made our work difficult. Now that we're better off, we still say the same. What's more, we said it doesn't pay to be a cadre. What contradiction does this notion reflect?"

The comrades discussed why they were always blaming their livelihood. Why did they always think they were "losing out" to be cadres? It was selfish ideas, they said, for during the early years of the liberation and agrarian reform they were all very enthusiastic despite the hard life. And during the early stage of agricultural co-operation it was the same. They firmly took the socialist road because they had suffered the bitterness of individual farming, and they held meetings, rain or shine. But now that their livelihood was better, the idea of "losing out" to be a cadre occurred to them. When meetings ran a little over the closing hour, some grumbled, felt tired, and that it was too much for them.

Secretary Chiang Ju-wang (middle) telling about his study of Chairman Mao's philosophic works.

What was the real reason for this? Why did they think more of personal interests and feel it "a loss" to them to be cadres when they were well off? What had they really lost?

A contradiction was there indeed, and it was selfish ideas that gave rise to the contradiction. They realized that it was a reflection of the struggle in their minds between the two roads, and happened when a person did not view himself from the standpoint of one dividing into two. Such a person saw only that he wanted to make revolution, but neglected the danger of taking the wrong road, thought only of his good class origin, but ignored the bourgeois ideas that endangered his thinking. Through such analysis, the Party branch cadres could calmly think over the critical remarks the brigade members had made.

They cited another example, that of an old cadre of sixty who had been very active during the years of agrarian reform. After agricultural co-operation, when production mounted steadily and his livelihood improved, he began to have a different view of life. He thought of the humiliating life he had led in the old society. Chairman Mao had rescued him from his bitter suffering and he could now enjoy himself. He built a new house after the liberation, while formerly he had had no house of his own. But now he thought it inadequate. There was accommodation for his sons, but scarcely enough for his grandsons as they grew up. Every day he strolled around his house, looking for space where additional rooms could be built for his grandsons. And so his self concern grew. Many brigade members criticized his way of thinking, but he turned a deaf ear. His case served a warning to all.

Another question arose. Which aspect of the contradiction was the principal one, granted the struggle between the two roads was the main contradiction? At first some said the principal aspect of the contradiction was those persons taking the capitalist road.

Then they studied and discussed fully the theory of the principal aspect of a contradiction in Chairman Mao's article. The working class and poor and lower-middle peasants were now the masters and in the dominant position, so they, the cadres, were the principal aspect of the contradiction — the leadership was the key. Once the principal aspect was grasped, there was the solution to the contradiction. As cadres, the Party committee members must never forget the poor and lower-middle peasants, wield power well on their behalf and prevent the class enemy from restoring capitalism.

The discussions solved the problem, as they established the cadres themselves as the principal aspect of the contradiction and refuted the idea that "it doesn't pay to be a cadre". Thus the cadres became more enthusiastic in their work.

The discussions solved the problem, as they established the cadres themselves as the principal aspect of the contradiction and refuted the idea that "it doesn't pay to be a cadre". Thus the cadres became more enthusiastic in their work.

The thirteen plots of land in the production brigade used to be short of water. But now the problem had in the main been solved, and rice could be double-cropped. All that should be done seemed to have been done. Average annual grain yield per mu in 1963 surpassed the targets set in the National Program for Agricultural Development, and the next year it jumped to 824 *jin*. Many cadres said: "We've reached the production peak; the yield can't go higher."

The Party branch got hold of this problem and started a discussion. Chiang Ju-wang said, " *'On Contradiction'* tells us that everything is in the process of development. It's metaphysical and wrong to see things as isolated and static. So, let's adopt this viewpoint of development to analyze the idea that 'production has reached its maximum' and see whether it's sound."

They contrasted the past with the present. Cadres who had doubted whether the brigade could get 800 *jin* of grain per mu now saw that the target was not only fulfilled but surpassed. Why had they doubted it then? It was because they thought wrongly that "production is at the maximum". Actually there is no limit to the production potential. The principal aspect of the contradiction was arrived at through such an analysis. They thought back over their experience and drew lessons: there were still many weak points in production, and much work remained to be done. The fertilizer was insufficient, the seeds needed improving, the double-crop rice acreage should be expanded, irrigation work had yet to be improved, etc., etc. After the brigade had done all this, production rose greatly in 1965, the grain yield jumping to 914 *jin* per *mu*.

Seeing the fruitful results of the study of philosophy, the masses took pride in saying: "Chairman Mao's '*On Contradiction*' really works." A member of the Party branch recalled how, at the beginning of the philosophy study they were said to be like tigers, unable to climb a tree. "But we were determined to do it, and now we've reached the first branch. With more effort we'll go higher."

Coverage of philosophic study by wall newspaper run by commune members.

MOVEMENT OF STUDYING PHILOSOPHY MOUNTS

Reason For Oddities Revealed

The Chinchien Production Brigade Party branch started studying philosophy in 1964, with twelve members taking part. Later, some activists were admitted, and the number increased to over twenty. But, at that time, the higher leadership did not encourage their study, so they kept it secret. After half a year, however, word of their study got out and spread. Every time Chiang Ju-wang went to a commune meeting, someone would say half in jest: "Oho, Veteran handler of contradictions', so here you are! Help me tackle my problems." Hearing the Chinchien Brigade members' arguments during work breaks, peasants of other brigades said grinning: "Why have you still so many problems after studying '*On Contradiction*'?" Thus they often chided Chiang and the comrades.

At that time there were many objective difficulties. Liu Shao-chi limited the publication of Chairman Mao's works to oppose the spread of Mao Zedong Thought. There were only four sets of *Selected Works of Mao Zedong* in the Chinchien Production Brigade, and all efforts to buy more from the Hsinhua bookstore in the county town failed. Nor was county authorization available for getting copies from Chinhua and Hangchow cities. It was an odd thing that the purchase of Chairman Mao's works should be restricted!

But that's not all.

Party member Chiang Cheng-liang had toiled for the landlords twenty-nine years in the old society, and had profound proletarian feelings for Chairman Mao. Though he was illiterate, he was determined to study philosophy. He lost three nights' sleep trying to fathom the meaning of "one divides into two". With the help of Chiang Ju-wang, Chiang Cheng-liang had begun reviewing his thinking and work in the light of one dividing into two. He thought: When China suffered temporary economic difficulties between 1960 and 1962, I lost much of my concern for the collective interest. I hoed my private plot energetically, but on the collective land it was another thing. I hoed with two kinds of energy — one for the collective and the other for myself. Aren't these in contradiction? It reflected the struggle in my mind between the two roads and the two ways of thinking. From then on, Chiang Cheng-liang always tried to be first in fighting self and criticizing revisionism, always putting the collective interest first. The poor and lower middle peasants said he studied well, and elected him to represent the poor and lower-middle peasants association at a province-level meeting. Chiang Cheng-liang told how he applied Chairman Mao's philosophic concepts to practice. The masses praised his speech and suggested that it should be published in the press. The manuscript went to a capitalist-roader in the propaganda department under the former provincial Party committee, who read it and shook his head. "I don't believe that an illiterate peasant can study so well!" he said, and suppressed the article.

It was the first half of 1965 that this capitalist-roader poured cold water on the Chinchien Production Brigade's study of Chairman Mao's philosophic works.

Then came the Great Proletarian Cultural Revolution. Responding to the great call of Chairman Mao's

Big-character poster "Bombard the Headquarters", hundreds of millions of revolutionary people throughout the country launched an attack on the bourgeois headquarters represented by the renegade, hidden traitor and scab Liu Shao-chi, and exposed his crimes one after another. Chiang Ju-wang and other comrades then understood that it was Liu Shao-chi who had been the taproot for restoring capitalism; it was he who ordered large numbers of co-operatives to be closed down, and who fanned up the evil trend of *san zi yi bao*. It was he who undermined the great socialist education movement by pushing his bourgeois reactionary line which was "Left" in form but Right in essence, and who opposed the mass movement to study and apply Chairman Mao's works.

Through the Great Proletarian Cultural Revolution, Chiang Ju-wang and his comrades understood better the inner-Party struggle between Chairman Mao's proletarian revolutionary line and Liu Shao-chi's counter-revolutionary revisionist line, and they heightened their consciousness of the struggle between them. Chiang Juwang realized that Liu and his agents in philosophical circles such as Yang Hsien-chen opposed the study of philosophy by workers, peasants and soldiers. The masses were proved to be right. Firmly responding to Chairman Mao's great call to *"liberate philosophy from the confines of the philosophers' lecture rooms and textbooks, and turn it into a sharp weapon in the hands of the masses"*, the people determined to push forward the mass movement to study philosophy.

To the Fore in Class Struggle

The struggle between the two classes, two roads and two lines in the Great Proletarian Cultural Revolution grew tense in the autumn of 1967. Just at this crucial moment the Chinchien Production Brigade was hit by an unusually serious drought and all the four reservoirs and eighty-three ponds dried up. The soil in the rice paddies became rock-hard and most of the late autumn crops withered. The situation seemed desperate.

Some people lost heart. "We're done for!" they wailed. "Even oxen won't eat fodder like that! How about us?"

Others said, "We have lost the autumn crop. And there is no hope to sow winter wheat on such hard soil. What will we eat next year!"

Some young people felt helpless in the face of these difficulties. Some wanted to go out to relatives or friends for help, while most of the old people intended to wait for state relief.

A handful of class enemies thought their chance had come, and they stepped out to fan up dissatisfaction. They spread it about that though the rice had withered, the people were not dead; they should use their wits to find a way out! These fellows started speculating and profiteering. Besides, they huddled together to gamble. Some went so far as to reverse the correct decisions passed on them. Underestimating the masses, they thought the people would be helpless before the natural calamity. And since cadres had been criticized and brushed aside, they thought they were free to "fish in troubled waters".

Facing these contradictions, Chiang Ju-wang thought: "The rice is dying from the drought. But the people are still alive. We must arm the masses with Chairman Mao's philosophic thinking and fight against the handful of class enemies. We must overcome the natural disaster by relying on our own efforts!"

The light burned late in the Chinchien Brigade, as the brigade leading members were having a meeting. Sitting around a table, Chiang Ju-wang, Tai Hsiang-mei, Chiang Fa-liang and other comrades were studying Chairman Mao's works. They had all received some criticism during the Great Proletarian Cultural Revolution, and some had just criticized themselves before the masses. They were becoming stronger, and closed their ranks further in times of trial.

Now they were analyzing the current ideas emerging in the brigade and came to the conclusion that varying as these ideas were, all essentially reflected the struggle between the two lines. Chiang Ju-wang observed that the ordinary brigade members had not yet started studying philosophy, though the Party branch had started in 1964. What the cadres understood was not necessarily understood by the masses; at the same time the cadres lacked a lot of knowledge that the masses had. The cadres would not achieve anything if they divorced themselves from the masses in their study. We must now grasp the key questions in the struggle between the two lines which concern everyone at present, and carry on an extensive study and debate. This would propagate Chairman Mao's philosophic thinking among the masses and stimulate the study of Chairman Mao's philosophic works.

The leading body discussed, and decided that attention should center on the principal contradiction. To combat the natural disaster, there must first be struggle against the class enemies. The people must be armed with Chairman Mao's philosophic thinking, so that correct views took root among the cadres and masses on main and side trends, good things and bad, mind and matter, and strengthened their determination to rely on their own efforts, work hard, defy difficulties and win victories. The Party members and the leadership must come to the fore in the sharp struggle between the two lines.

But a handful of class enemies in the neighborhood set out to undermine the brigade's mass movement to study and apply Chairman Mao's works. One of these enemies said, "It was claimed there was no gambling or speculation in the brigade. I don't believe it. Now persons in power like Chiang Ju-wang and Tai Hsiangmei have to behave themselves. I had not gone in for gambling at Chinchien, but now I'll go and have a try."

This handful of class enemies, who had been drinking, met at a bad person's house in the brigade.

That afternoon, a lad reported to the brigade leading group that several drunken characters from an unknown place were gambling there. They called themselves members of a so-called "Iron Bastion Fighting Team".

A challenge from class enemies! Chiang Ju-wang and his comrades made up their minds to take up the challenge and repulse these class enemies. They would need to be both bold and careful. In the light of Chairman Mao's teaching on investigation and study, Ju-wang sent some brigade members to check on the situation. What kind of people were these anyway?

The members went and took a look and recognized the drunken gamblers at once. "One is supposed to be under surveillance by a people's commune," announced one who was doing the checking. "I know that fellow," said another. "He's a known speculator in a village more than ten *li* (1/2 kilometer) away."

Thus the pack of gamblers were identified for what they were. The brigade leaders called on the masses to surround the house, and six shady characters were brought out and a struggle meeting was held on the spot. Sweating under the scrutiny of the masses, this handful of class enemies confessed to their criminal activities of corruption, theft and speculation.

But the class enemies did not give in. Frightened by the blow the Chinchien peasant masses had dealt them, they changed to secret activities. They spread rumors about how strong they were in numbers, and that they were going to wipe out the Chinchien Brigade and do away with Chiang Ju-wang. Ju-wang's wife was worried at this threat. But the masses of the poor and lower-middle peasants said to her: "Don't worry. We all stand by him." Chiang realized that the fight against the enemy took precedence over the fight

Against nature, and that he must fight self before fighting the enemy. This was to be a severe test. He must put daring above all else, and fight the enemy resolutely. The leading group organized a propaganda team to expose the enemy's schemes by propagating Chairman Mao's teachings on class struggle. The enemies wrote anonymous letters to Chiang and others, while they replied by putting up open letters to the handful of enemies. After some time these bad elements decamped and hid in a gully on the border between Chekiang and Kiangsi provinces, imagining they would be safe there, as they could run into Kiangsi Province and claim they belonged there in case the Chekiang peasants went after them. They would reverse their direction and story if the peasants of Kiangsi tried to capture them. But it was not like that. With the help of the poor and lowermiddle peasants of other brigades, the revolutionary masses of Chinchien soon took them into custody. There was only a dozen of them — a mere handful of the dregs of society disguised as the "Iron Bastion Fighting Team" — which collapsed once the masses got together to struggle against them.

Big Argument and Hard Struggle

Chiang Ju-wang and others of the brigade leading group determined to follow up the victory over the class enemy. They called the brigade members together to study Chairman Mao's philosophic concepts in preparation for the fight against nature with the same revolutionary spirit as in fighting against the class enemy.

At the meeting, all discussed enthusiastically the struggle against class enemies, and how they had smashed them. "A good lesson to those scoundrels, eh?" said someone. But when they talked about the situation of the brigade, many expressed lack of confidence in overcoming the natural difficulties.

Chiang Chien-wen, brigade instructor in Chairman Mao's works, stood and read the following teaching of Chairman Mao: *"The way these comrades look at problems is wrong. They do not look at the essential or main aspects but emphasize the non-essential or minor ones"*

Then the instructor said: "I think some comrades are concentrating on minor aspects. We must make over-all analysis and see the situation as a whole. For example, we used to have only four sets of *Selected Works of Mao Zedong* and not a single copy of *Quotations from Chairman Mao Zedong*. We spent a lot of time copying down the quotations by hand. Now everyone of us has books by Chairman Mao and never before has Mao Zedong Thought been disseminated on such a big scale. Isn't the situation very encouraging?"

Someone added: "That's right. The masses have been mobilized, and Liu Shao-chi has been overthrown. The situation is really excellent."

"By the way," Chiang Chien-wen continued, "the class enemy's coming out into the open was not bad, but a good thing, which has been proved by our own experience. We just smashed the demons one after another and tempered ourselves in the struggle."

Through the day-long discussion, the brigade members began to have a clear idea about the general situation. Then they switched to the question of how to overcome the current difficulties.

An old production team leader stood up, pipe in hand, and said aloud: "I say we should still put politics in command. When we had insect pests in 1964, the other production teams suffered little loss because they worked hard to eliminate the pests while our team slackened its effort and didn't bring the human factor into full play and this brought big losses of our rice crop. We must have politics in command."

Tai Hsiang-mei surveyed the brigade members and said: "This used to be a poverty-stricken place, and that was a bad thing; but poverty gives rise to the desire for change. After working hard and making revolution, we had good harvests year after year and ended the backwardness. We turned a bad thing into a good one, but we became complacent and neglected water conservancy construction and now we are suffering for it. In this case we turned the good thing into a bad one." She continued in strong voice: "Our discussion today is aimed at changing this bad thing back into a good one."

The instructor again led the poor and lower-middle peasants in studying Chairman Mao's teaching: "*We must learn to look at problems all-sidedly, seeing the reverse as well as the obverse side of things. In given conditions, a bad thing can lead to good results and a good thing to bad results.*" Chiang Ju-wang illustrated this in the light of local conditions.

Filled with confidence, the brigade members acknowledged that their difficulties were really great: the water had dried up, the land was parched and the rice-seedlings dead. However, while making the people suffer, the drought put them to the test. It was like the soil. On the one hand it was hardened by the sun; on the other it was good for cultivation, having been fallowed. In given conditions, a bad thing can be transformed into a good thing and disadvantages into advantages. So long as the poor and lower-middle peasants follow Chairman Mao's teachings and are united, they will overcome not only the class enemy but also natural disasters.

Revolutionary mass criticism followed. The poor and lower-middle peasants pointed out that the two different attitudes towards difficulties were, in essence, a reflection of the two world outlooks and the struggle between the two lines. Either going out to friends and relatives for help or seeking aid from the government was no way out.

The only correct way to surmount difficulties and transform bad things into good ones was by relying on the collective and working hard in the spirit of self-reliance.

After three days and evenings of studies and discussions, the brigade members' thinking was unified around Chairman Mao's philosophic concepts, and early the next morning they hoisted the board inscribed with this quotation from Chairman Mao: "Be resolute, fear no sacrifice and surmount every difficulty to win victory." They set about fighting nature, with hoe, water-pail and shoulder pole. When the land was too hard for the ploughs, they turned it up with hoes. They carried water from a distance in pails on shoulder poles. The leading cadres such as Chiang Ju-wang and Tai Hsiang-mei got up earliest in the morning, returned home latest and always encouraged the brigade members. They said: "As we carry water in a fight against drought, we are following the revolutionary line of Chairman Mao. Victory is ours if we stick it out."

After two weeks of hard struggle, the land was covered with green wheat seedlings.

Once, when the peasants were studying philosophy in the fields, Chiang Ju-wang asked: "Where did these seedlings come from?"

The leading cadre of the 3rd production team answered: "They're sprouts from our study of Chairman Mao's teaching of self-reliance and hard work."

The leader of the 9th team added: "They're also sprouts from our study of Chairman Mao's philosophic writings and of our own hard work."

Chiang Ju-wang summed up by saying: "Yes, Chairman Mao's philosophic thinking directing our effort in conquering nature yielded a good crop on dry land. This is just what Chairman Mao teaches, 'from matter to consciousness and then back to matter'. Once Mao Zedong Thought arms our minds, it results in a tremendous material force."

"Oh! So this is what is called from consciousness to matter!" the peasants realized. Many of them had heard of it before, but they had not really understood it. Now they recognized it through the crop they planted and their efforts to fight nature.

In the course of the struggle between the two lines in combating drought the poor and lower-middle peasants came to grasp such philosophic concepts as the major aspect and minor aspect of a thing, good and bad things changing place, from matter to consciousness and back to matter.

A new upsurge of the mass movement for studying philosophy was developing in depth.

"We Have the Spiritual Atomic Bomb!"

In the winter of 1967, the brigade Party branch decided the Hsunung reservoir should be enlarged. Construction of the reservoir started before the Great Proletarian Cultural Revolution, but the work went ahead very slowly because the leadership paid exclusive attention to the results brought by the hoe, and failed to grasp man's thinking and put proletarian politics in command. What's more, it tried to speed up the work by "putting pay in command". Therefore a lot of disputes arose around the payment of work-points on the construction site. After seven winters, the reservoir had a capacity of only 80,000 cubic meters. The brigade Party branch committee members studied Chairman Mao's philosophic thinking and summed up their positive and negative experience. They saw that the hoe and man's thinking are opposites, and that man is the principal aspect of the contradiction. The hoe is wielded by man, so in order to make the hoe work well it is necessary to grasp man's thinking first. Only by using Mao Zedong Thought to educate people can the hoe be fully used.

After a joint discussion, the Party branch committee members, cadres and masses decided that in rebuilding the reservoir, they would put proletarian politics in command and ideological work first. They decided to turn the construction site into a battlefield for revolutionary mass criticism and a classroom for the study of Chairman Mao's works.

It was very cold that winter, but the construction site was bubbling with activity. More than two hundred men and women brigade members gathered to criticize the counter-revolutionary revisionist line of the renegade, hidden traitor and scab Liu Shao-chi, his hogwash, "put pay in command" and material incentives. After fostering the concept of farming for the revolution, the brigade members voluntarily started work at half past six instead of at eight in the morning. During work breaks, they gathered together and sang revolutionary songs.

One day a comrade from a neighboring village was amazed by the scene as he passed by. He asked in astonishment: "Your brigade was hit by such a serious drought, but you people are working with such energy. How's that?"

A young peasant answered proudly: "We have the spiritual atomic bomb, that is, we're armed with Mao Zedong Thought!"

Dialectics enabled the peasants to conquer nature. They took only forty days to complete 140,000 cubic metres of earthwork originally scheduled to take two months. This topped the total done in the previous seven years by a wide margin.

The hard labor of the winter of 1967 brought rich results the next year. Then another dry spell of more than a hundred days hit. The grain yield per mu came to 994 *jin* that drought year.

Recalling their experiences, the poor and lower middle peasants of the brigade often say: "Our brigade began to study philosophy in the struggle between the two lines and brought about a new upsurge in the mass movement for the study. The sharper the struggle between the two lines, the more we saw the effect of philosophy — our keen weapon. If we peasants study philosophy in the light of the problems everyone is concerned about in the struggle between the two lines, we can understand it quickly and apply it well — just like dry soil absorbing raindrops."

Bumper harvest despite serious drought.

CONSTANTLY MORE AWARE OF CLASS STRUGGLE

"We Chaings Are All One Family!"

Chinchien Production Brigade started purifying its class ranks in 1968. In this complex struggle against the class enemy, the poor and lower-middle peasants of the brigade gained a better understanding of Chairman Mao's philosophic thinking.

A few people had not been vigilant, not aware of the enemy's presence. Someone said, "We've lived in this village for generations and are crystal clear what had happened here both before and after the liberation. Besides, we know all the former landlords and rich peasants by name." True, nine out of ten brigade members have the same surname, Chiang. This was a fact the class enemy seized on to spread feudal patriarchal notions. "We Chiangs spring from a common root. We're all one family," they said, trying to hoodwink the people and shield themselves. Some people were poisoned by the class enemy and chimed in: "We Chiangs are all one family and meet every day. We should plant flowers together, not thistles, and keep a good clan relationship."

Success in purifying the class ranks meant exposing the class enemy's tricks and raising the people's awareness of class struggle. The brigade Party branch ran various classes to study Chairman Mao's teachings, "Contradiction is universal and absolute" and "Never forget class struggle", and criticized Liu Shao-chi's theory of "the dying out of class struggle".

People came to realize that in class society there is only class love, and no patriarchal love. Now the class enemy was trying by cunning means to establish family connections with us. Why, in the old days when they exploited and oppressed us, didn't they talk about our family ties? Now they appeared very close to us; actually it was all a hoax to pacify us. We must not relax our vigilance.

Many poor and lower-middle peasants related experiences in the old society as lessons to the younger generation that feudal patriarchal ideas must be smashed.

One evening after work, the old poor peasant of the 11th team Chiang Chun-cheng was returning home with his daughter Mei-lan when the ex-landlord, whom people called "pig bristles", swaggered past their house. Chun-cheng was infuriated at the sight of him and referred to him as the "pig bristles" landlord. Perplexed, the little girl enquired: "But isn't he my granduncle? Why do you call him such names?"

Pointing at him behind his back, her father replied: "He may be your grandfather's brother, but he's not one of us!"

Mei-lan was more confused. Why was this relative not of their family? "Father, when I was working in the fields I heard people say that those with the same surname belong to the same family. Why doesn't this granduncle belong to ours?"

Hearing this, Chun-cheng was enraged. He recalled that such ideas as the Chiangs being all one family, planting flowers but not thistles, etc., had been spread about since the class ranks had begun to be purified, and all these tricks were played by the enemy to damage the movement. Because his daughter had been taken in by such talk, he decided to make things clear, and so he told her the unforgettable story of their family.

Chiang Chun-cheng's father had died when he was twelve, and he lived with his mother and two younger sisters in misery, with no way out. Finally his younger sister was sold as a child bride.

To top it all, the "pig bristles" landlord, abusing his power, seized Chiang Chun-cheng's house and vegetable garden and wanted to lay hands on his only plot of land.

The landlord went to Chiang Chun-cheng and, in a show of pity, said to him: "Your life is hard and I can't bear to see you go hungry. I'll bring you some grain and you let me use your land." Then, not even waiting for an answer, "pig bristles" left. A few days later it was going around that Chun-cheng had sold his plot of land, though there was no title deed. Anyway, the landlord sent his men to till the land. Chun-cheng was angry and wanted to reason with him, but the avaricious landlord forgot about being of the same "family". He brought a suit before the county court, charging Chuncheng with "illegal occupancy". Gazing at the summons, Chun-cheng was so shocked that he spat blood. He remembered the saying: The door of the court is wide open, but not to those who have no money though they are in the right. He knew that going to court meant fines or imprisonment for him. Later Chun-cheng was forced to work as a hired hand for that landlord till years of hard labor bent his back.

With the liberation, the Party and Chairman Mao rescued Chun-cheng from his misery, and he stood up and struggled against the landlord, whose property was confiscated and divided up among the poor and lower middle peasants. But his reactionary thinking could not be confiscated, and he never stopped plotting a comeback. Even during the Great Proletarian Cultural Revolution, he never missed a chance to sneak into houses that had been shared out to check whether the columns and beams were wormy, dreaming of getting the houses back. Chun-cheng had found him doing this and struggled against him face to face.

"So you see," said Chiang Chun-cheng to his daughter, "the Chiangs are divided into two. Some were landlords before, others were poor and lower-middle peasants. Most of the Chiangs are now taking the socialist road, but some prefer capitalism.

The two kinds are not of the same family but are hostile to each other. 'All one family' is a reactionary idea spread by the class enemy, who fears being exposed by the revolutionary people. So don't be fooled! To consolidate the dictatorship of the proletariat, we must struggle hard against such class enemies."

Beware the Dog That Doesn't Bark

Among those who spread the "all one family" idea was a landlord by the name of Chiang Jui-lu. He had been away for a long time and returned to the village in 1948. After the land reform in 1950, he began to take part in farm production under the supervision of the masses. He looked submissive enough, and even very energetic in labor. He never quarreled with anybody. He appeared to be studying farm technique assiduously, and subscribed to a newspaper as if he were very diligent. Sometimes he even offered to treat sick peasants and supply them with medicines. Brigade members began to feel that this landlord had reformed quite well, and they relaxed their vigilance against him.

But, when purification of the class ranks began, the brigade members under the guidance of Chairman Mao's philosophic ideas brought out contradictions and stated facts. With everybody thinking and discussing, suspicion soon focused on Chiang Jui-lu. The people said: "In judging whether class enemies are honest or not, we must look not only at appearance but see what's inside, and see the essence through the appearance. In considering action and ideology, we must differentiate between cases and treat them accordingly. Those who admitted their misdeeds and worked honestly should be dealt with lightly; those who appeared honest but schemed and sneaked about behind people's backs should be struggled against. What was the true character of Chiang Jui-lu? They analyzed his case and found many contradictory facts.

Some pointed out that he had been away for a long time before liberation, and who knew what he had done all those years? And why was it that although he returned full of important airs, he would never breathe a word about his past to anyone?

Others added that when he returned he was only forty-two, yet he raised a beard even longer than his father's. Why did he want to appear old?

The more questions were raised and analyzed, the more suspicion grew. There was an old saying at Kiangshan County that went: *"A barking dog may bite, but more vicious is the bite of the dog that doesn't bark."* You are warned by the dog that barks, while those that don't, bite you unawares. Chairman Mao teaches us: *"When we look at a thing, we must examine its essence and treat its appearance merely as an usher at the threshold, and once we cross the threshold, we must grasp the essence of the thing."* But there is true appearance and false appearance. Chairman Mao also warns us against counter-revolutionaries in disguise that "conceal their true features by giving a false impression. But since they oppose the revolution, it is impossible for them to cover up their true features completely." Chiang Jui-lu was one of these: though he tried to give people an impression of honesty, he gave himself away in many places.

Someone reported seeing Chiang secretly send off a suitcase and wondered what was in it.

The leading group called on the people to track the suitcase down, and they soon located it in a train station three li away. It was found to contain incriminating documents — certificates of appointments, orders of transfer, etc. the Kuomintang reactionaries had issued to him before the liberation.

It outlined a counter-revolutionary history steeped in crime. Here indeed was a fierce dog that didn't bark!

Since the evidence was at hand, Chiang Jui-lu was summoned for questioning. Thinking his suitcase was already far away and the leading group knew nothing about it, he admitted nothing when asked about his crimes, but repeated over and over, sighing: "If I'm really guilty of any crime the people's government can have my head or shoot me if it likes." When evidence was produced and he could no longer deny the facts, he exclaimed: "Ah, so I've forgotten. I deserve to die. Let the government punish me." When more evidence was produced, it was the same thing all over again. He would sigh: "There's no more. If any crime is discovered the government can punish me as it likes."

Some people thought this person's crimes were all exposed and there was nothing more to investigate. Chiang Ju-wang disagreed. "We'd better look further into this case. He's still holding back. And have we found out everything? We should not be too ready to believe his confessions."

Three months later, someone discovered a Browning pistol he had buried in his vegetable garden. Faced with this, he sighed again: "Ah, I deserve to die. I buried it there, but that's all. Let the government do with me as it likes." So it was again and again. The leading group didn't take his admission too seriously but continued to investigate. They dug up a dagger and ammunition.

This round in the class battle helped people see the complexity of class struggle and understand better the relationship between the essence of a thing and its appearance. They carried forward the movement to purify the class ranks and exposed some other class enemies.

While Paying Attention to One Trend ,
Don't Neglect Another, Possibly Hidden

However, in the excellent situation, a new and different tendency claimed attention. When Chinchien Production Brigade brought to light a Kuomintang army major unknown for many years, someone exulted: "Good! We've found a major; now for the lieutenant colonel! There must be a lieutenant-colonel since there's a major."

The masses were aroused and gave evidence against several people, but most of it was inconclusive. Chiang Ju-wang and the other brigade leaders sat down and made a serious study of Chairman Mao's relevant works. ". . . *Right deviations must be combated where the masses have not yet been aroused in earnest and the struggle has not yet unfolded, and 'Left 5 deviations must be guarded against where the masses have been aroused in earnest and the struggle has already unfolded."*

With this quotation from Chairman Mao as criterion, they discussed their progress in purifying the class ranks. Chiang Ju-wang took full notes and thought the situation over carefully. "That's it," he concluded. "We must guard against 'Left' deviations, for the people have been aroused. Discovering a major doesn't necessarily mean there's a lieutenant-colonel. I think that's idealism."

The comrades agreed and decided that in dealing with suspects, the Party's proletarian policy should be strictly carried out. Stress should be laid on the weight of evidence and on investigation and study.

After that, some people accused the brigade cadres of "Right deviation", of "shelving the cases of established counter-revolutionaries". But the comrades countered these accusations with the firm answer:

Strictly carrying out Party policy is a vital question of Party spirit and of carrying out Chairman Mao's revolutionary line."

They began deep-going and careful investigation and study. Prior to investigation they felt muddled, but once investigation had been made things became very clear. Basing on the investigation results and guided by the Party policy, the brigade leaders made an all-round study of each person suspected and strictly differentiated between the two types of contradictions, which were with the enemy and which were among the people.

In the brigade was a person with a counter-revolutionary history who had been shielded by a handful of capitalist roaders and hailed as an "education expert", "enlightened gentleman" and "deputy to the county people's congress". In purifying the class ranks the poor and lower-middle peasants investigated him, exposed contradictions and supplied evidence. With everybody thinking and discussing, they finally exposed this "revolutionary" as a long-time counter-revolutionary. They said: "We've caught a big fish. Purifying the class ranks has really brought results!" In deciding this counterrevolutionary's case, the brigade leaders considered his attitude in admitting his misdeeds and, after discussion with the poor and lower-middle peasants, dealt with him leniently and gave him a way out. Some started complaining that purifying the class ranks had resulted in nothing. "All our trouble has netted only one fat fish," they said, "and even that has been thrown back."

These few words attracted the brigade leaders' attention, and they promptly organized the peasants to discuss whether or not purifying the class ranks had been effective. Then, people realized that according to proletarian policy a person with a counter-revolutionary history must be given a way out in order better to supervise and reform him. Class enemies were thus soon disintegrated and some came clean, which substantially promoted the work of purifying the class ranks.

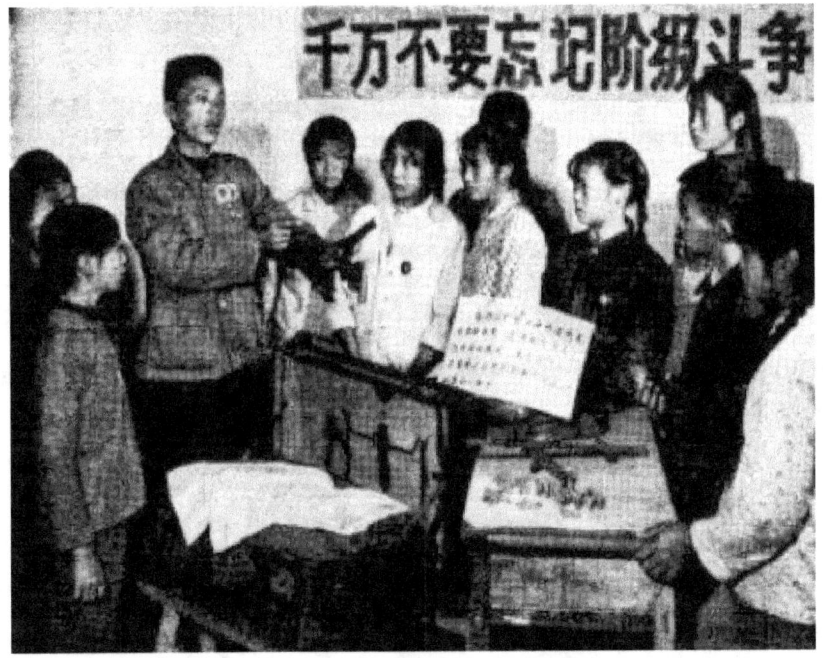

千万不要忘记阶级斗争

The brigade militia company commander cites crimes of the landlord Chiang Jui-lu as negative examples to educate the youth.

The result could be judged not only by the number of enemies exposed, but by whether proletarian dictatorship had been consolidated.

Some cases had been decided, but the class struggle never ceased. The members of Chinchien Brigade continued probing for class enemies, while at the same time relentlessly denouncing those class enemies who dared to reverse their cases by taking advantage of our implementation of Party policy.

Led by the Party branch, the poor and lower-middle peasants kept their eyes on the main tendency without ignoring different hidden ones. They guarded against disturbances from the ultra "Left" while combating Right trends, and vice versa. In this way, the movement of struggle-criticism-transformation proceeded successfully along Chairman Mao's revolutionary line.

To Carry a Gun Without Seeing a Bird, or to Have a Bird but No Gun?

In spring of 1970 a movement began to strike at counter-revolutionaries and to oppose corruption and theft, speculation, extravagance and waste.

Mass discussion revealed that some comrades were unjustifiably complacent. They questioned whether there was anything to be "struck at" or "opposed" in this brigade, since it was an advanced unit with a strong core of leadership and good mass base, the class ranks had been purified and proletarian dictatorship consolidated. To carry on class struggle now would be like "carrying a gun without seeing a bird".

Then Chiang Ken-tu, brigade Party branch member, presided over a meeting at which he said: "We of Chinchien are used to talking things over and have found discussion a good method in studying philosophy. When a problem arose, the people analyzed it in the light of Chairman Mao's philosophic works and it became very clear. Today we're going to discuss whether it is right or wrong to say that we're carrying a gun when there's no bird."

An old poor peasant of the 8th team was the first to speak. "I'm not a good student of philosophy and really have no argument. But I'd like to say something about my son. He was born in the new society, grew up under the red flag and knew nothing of class struggle. He said that if he beat a tiger he'd rather beat a live one; if he ate fish he'd prefer a fat carp, that there was nothing to be hit because all the tigers were dead." The old peasant's anger mounted as he went on: "That scoundrel that's been here working under mass supervision was talking to my son just a few days ago, dampening his enthusiasm for work. He said to the young fellows working on the threshing floor:

You break those wicker scoops working so hard. How many scoops and hoes can you earn by your one year's hard labor!' Influenced by him, my son left his wicker scoop behind that afternoon and just idled the time away. Besides, he said he was carrying a gun when there was no bird. Why, I think he wouldn't know if a bird alighted on his head!" The old man sat down quite out of breath.

Chiang Ken-tu commented that the old poor peasant was right. What we want a discussion to do is present the facts, reason things out, expose the fresh activities of the class enemy and disprove the notion that we're carrying a gun when there's no bird!"

A woman stood up and continued: "I'd like to say a few words. The woman ex-landowner in our brigade went to the field yesterday. She worked a while, stopped a while and rested herself, and did a little more. Then she gazed at the sky, heaved a sigh, and muttered to herself: I was born under an unlucky star. If I wasn't, I wouldn't be sweating here; I'd be fanning myself and looking after my grandsons at home.' Now, this woman ex-landowner wants to restore capitalism, doesn't she? Yesterday the women of the 5th team criticized her severely for spreading superstition, talking about Luck', while not reforming herself honestly. Does she mean to say a person with good Luck' can go on exploiting others?"

The speaker was followed by others with similar exposures of the class enemy. A commune member of the 4th team rose and began: "Our team's 'quiet dog' Chiang Jui-lu, has become rabid and shown his fangs. He not only slipped out of surveillance but also poisoned the relations between cadres and masses. . . ."

The commune members became more incensed with each exposure. Accusations followed, and pledges were made. Facts had refuted the fallacy of "carrying a gun when there was no bird".

However, the comrades of the Chinchien Brigade Party branch did not feel that enough had been done.

They were always consciously raising the masses'
understanding to a higher philosophic level, and studied philosophy
in the light of the practical struggle. Chiang Ken-tu led the
comrades in studying a quotation from Chairman Mao:
*"Contradiction is universal and absolute, it is present in the process of
development of all things and permeates every process from beginning
to end."* Ken-tu went on: "Everybody can talk about the universality of contradiction, but talking is one thing and applying is
another. Applying well here doesn't mean applying well somewhere
else. Being able to apply yesterday doesn't mean you can do it
today. There are some who talk about the universality of
contradiction while at the same time refusing to recognize the contradictions existing in this advanced brigade. In class society, where
are there no class contradictions, no class struggle? Are those
comrades who talk about 'carrying a gun without seeing a bird'
really carrying a gun? Not at all. They say they're carrying a gun,
while actually they've already thrown it away."

Ken-tu's analysis deepened the comrades' understanding of
the universality of contradiction, so that the discussion became
more lively and intense.

"Well, I think an advanced brigade is advanced not because
there is no class struggle, but in consciously grasping it."

"That's it! How can a brigade be advanced if it doesn't grasp
class struggle!"

"Proletarian dictatorship is firm in our brigade as a whole, but
there are bound to be some places where it's not so firm. A thing
can always divide into two."

Gradually the people were talking along the same lines. The
poor and lower-middle peasants remarked: "After a bee dies its
sting still poisons people; when a snake dies its tail still coils three
times; when a class enemy is overthrown he still wants to put up a
last-ditch struggle. Class struggle must be grasped every year, every
month and every day, must never be relaxed for a single moment."

The discussion had brought Chairman Mao's philosophic ideas into the very hearts of the people and, with eyes open, they deepened and expanded the movement to strike at counter-revolutionaries and oppose corruption and theft, speculation, extravagance and waste.

LEADERS TAKE THE LEAD IN STUDY AND APPLICATION

Party Branch Secretary Who Studies and Applies Philosophy

People say the brigade Party branch secretary Chiang Ju-wang studies philosophy well. He is good at applying the materialist dialectical concept of "one dividing into two" in the three great revolutionary movements of class struggle, the struggle for production and scientific experiment. He is good at grasping the key link of the struggle between the two lines in correctly analyzing and handling various complex contradictions, and at using the sharp weapon of philosophy well to remold his own world outlook.

The brigade was cited at the end of 1969 as an advanced unit in the study of Mao Tsetung Thought for the whole province to emulate. Some brigade cadres thought that with new leaders and new leading body, and being an advanced unit, where was any two-line struggle? People kept coming to learn from Chinchien Production Brigade, but there were also comments from a few visitors that while the brigade rated very well in the study of philosophy it was not the best in production. These comments set Chiang Ju-wang on edge.

He found the early rice seedlings not growing very well in an advanced team and criticized the leader. "Your team will have to do better in production"

He said to the team leader, who was worried for fear his team would lose the honored title of advanced. Eager to increase output, he called for the application of more fertilizer, taking no account of objective conditions. As a result the rice lodged and output did not increase much. The brigade asked the masses what they thought was the cause. One peasant suggested that the leading body might look for the contradiction within itself. That made Chiang Ju-wang think, and he found he himself was responsible for it. He had the idea for a time that he had done a good job of political work and that he should concentrate on production. Thus he had slighted political work, which was precisely the cause. Through the discussion, Chiang Ju-wang and other comrades, too, saw more clearly what the relation was between politics and production. Production, which has to be grasped, must still be commanded by politics, and ideological work stressed. This is the correct line to be adopted. The idea of increasing output for the sole purpose of gaining honor is an expression of "putting production first" which inevitably leads to falling behind in both politics and production.

In leading the masses' study of philosophy in the past few years, Chiang Ju-wang and other members of the Party branch have found many good study methods and have gained experience, which includes debates and comparing experience in the study. Debates are often held, when various views are presented and backed up by passages from Chairman Mao's "*On Practice*", "*On Contradiction*" and his other works. Such meetings are so interesting that no one wants to leave a question over till next time, even when the meeting runs late into the night. Such debates have helped the commune members in their understanding and supplied many of the good ideas Chiang Ju-wang and others have later summed up. Whenever they meet a knotty problem, they say: "Well, when shall we call a meeting to debate the matter?"

At these meetings the floor is given chiefly to the main debaters elected by different teams and holding different views, while the rest sit listening or adding what their representative speakers leave out. Many problems are solved this way. Of course, the questions debated should be of concern to the majority.

Chiang Ju-wang is also good at bringing the role of the backbone members of the brigade into play, the brigade having organized a philosophy study group with the Party branch as core. In this is a writing group composed of brigade cadres, veteran poor peasants and young intellectuals, more than twenty in all. The three senior middle school graduates, invited by the Party branch in 1964 to coach the philosophy study class, also joined this writing group and, helped by the Party branch and poor and lower-middle peasants, gradually discarded the bad influence of their old education, and understood that theory must be combined with practice. Thus they made marked progress. This writing group played an important role in studying and coaching, as well as writing. Since 1964 it has produced more than 200 articles, many of them having appeared in the press.

Tai Hsiang-mei Studies Dialectics

Tai Hsiang-mei, woman deputy secretary of Chipchien Production Brigade Party branch, had suffered cruelly from the oppression and exploitation of the landlord class, and her bitter experience in the old society made her hate the class enemy very much. Chairman Mao had saved her. She had deep proletarian feeling for Chairman Mao and was very active in her work. Still, this active Party member also had her shortcomings when it came to solving problems of the collective.

Private plots are small pieces of land for commune members' individual use. One such plot was so situated that it interfered with the ploughing of a piece of collective land. So it was decided that this plot should be included in the collective land and another plot be allotted to the member. But this member was not pleased with the idea. Then, without explaining further to him, Tai Hsiang-mei and other commune members ploughed up the private plot, after which she allocated him another piece of land, assuming that everyone agreed that private interests are subordinate to the collective interest. The commune member was angry and, stamping his foot, shouted: "It's only what you leaders say that goes, is it? We ordinary members have no voice in anything!" Tai Hsiang-mei was taken aback. Strange! What was there to make such a fuss about?

Such occurrences were frequent, till some poor and lower-middle peasants went to her and said: "Hsiangmei, your ways are too arbitrary and crude." Secretary Chiang Ju-wang added: "It's not enough for us to be daring and decisive in revolutionary work, we must learn how to work well. And to work well we must study the dialectical method."

True, there were bound to be troubles in the world. Tai Hsiang-mei wanted to work with all her heart for the revolution, but it seemed she often hit her head against a stone wall. She couldn't understand why there were so many problems.

Then she studied philosophy and learned that problems mean contradictions, which exist everywhere. In making revolution, Communists must recognize contradictions and analyze and solve them. You can't just depend on enthusiasm, but must pay attention to method and rely on dialectics. Tai Hsiang-mei is no longer surprised or impatient when problems arise, but analyses them factually and tries to solve them.

Party branch deputy secretary Tai Hsiang-mei (middle) works in
the fields with commune members.

One day during harvesting a peasant looked around at the
rich crops and exclaimed with satisfaction: "Most of the work is
done. Now that we've reached the harvest, we can take it a little
easy."

Such a remark in the past would have brought a sharp rebuke
from Tai Hsiang-mei right then and there. But this time she said
nothing. After thinking over the remark, she asked him and a team
leader to look over an especially good field. "Do you think output
on this land will be increased or not?" she said.

"No doubt there'll be a good harvest," the team leader
replied, and estimated how big the increase would be.

Pointing to two rows of rice, Hsiang-mei said: "These were
eaten by rice borers. That cuts the output, doesn't it?"

They were discussing the matter when the commune member
Chiang Sheng-te said: "Well, two rows of rice is more than a
hundred bunches. Each bunch yields an ounce of grain; two rows
mean ten jin . If those two rows were not eaten by rice borers,
there'd be that much more rice."

"Right," Hsiang-mei said. "Everything divides into two, the main aspect and the minor one. In general, our harvest this year is good, and that's the main aspect. But still there are some losses. This is the minor aspect. We must concentrate on the main aspect and encourage the commune members. But we shouldn't ignore the minor aspect. We must understand that our work still has many shortcomings, and the main and minor aspects can change into each other. That is to say, if we don't pay attention to solving the minor aspect, it may become the main one. A bumper harvest is in sight, but if we don't work hard, we won't get it. How can we feel we may take it a little easy?"

All agreed this was true, and pledged not to slacken their efforts.

Hsiang-mei says: One cannot do his job well without dialectics, and if one wants to fight selfishness, he must also use dialectics.

In the early days of the Cultural Revolution, Tai Hsiang-mei was criticized by the masses and lost heart. She did not understand why this was, since she worked so hard for the revolution. Chiang Ju-wang talked to her and together they studied Chairman Mao's teaching: *"It is wrong to appraise our work either from the viewpoint that everything is positive, or from the viewpoint that everything is negative."* Ju-wang said: "We're Communist Party members and it's our duty to serve the people; there are certainly many mistakes in our work as cadres over the past years and we should correct them. We should look at ourselves from the viewpoint of one dividing into two." Tai Hsiang-mei thought back over her work and found that she had made many mistakes. Why had she not been conscious of her mistakes then? Wasn't it simply that she didn't look at the two aspects of herself? She thought only of her good class origin and enthusiasm for the revolution, but not of the influence of bourgeois ideas.

She paid attention only to reforming the objective world, neglecting to remold her own subjective outlook. A cadre who doesn't listen carefully to criticism may make a small mistake to start with, but which in the end leads people onto the wrong road and brings losses to the cause of the Party.

With this understanding, Hsiang-mei plucked up her courage and tried to fight her selfishness. In the interests of the people, she persists in doing what is right and corrects what is wrong. The poor and lower-middle peasants praise her for being tempered through revolutionizing her ideology. During the Party consolidation movement last year the masses had much less unfavorable criticism of her.

How did this Party cadre deal with her progress in thinking?

One evening after the brigade Party consolidation study class, Tai Hsiang-mei said to Chiang Ju-wang: "I'm uneasy about the Party consolidation this time."

"What's the matter?" asked Ju-wang.

"The masses had so little criticism of me. That's not good!"

"They didn't criticize me much either."

"I think we should analyze 'more' and 'less' criticism specifically. More criticism possibly means more shortcomings. But not necessarily. Less criticism doesn't necessarily mean less shortcomings. We have to analyze the nature of the criticism. More criticism may mean I have more shortcomings and mistakes, but it will help me correct them and further my ideological revolutionization; less criticism muddles me so I can't see my own shortcomings!"

"You're right," Chiang Ju-wang said. "Furthermore, more and less criticism transform into each other. Why do people have less criticism? Because you've made progress."

"But if I'm complacent and conceited, criticism will increase," she cut in.

Then Chiang Ju-wang went on: "We can't afford to be conceited even if people criticize us less. We will follow Chairman Mao and advance constantly if we persist in study and application of Chairman Mao's philosophic works, constantly analyze ourselves from the viewpoint of one dividing into two and continue to revolutionize our thinking!"

Chiang Chien-wei Does Frequent Weeding

The rice rippled and gleamed under the blue sky. The Chinchien Brigade 8th team members were harvesting.

Elated, one of the young fellows doing the cutting shouted: "Look! This issue of Red Flag carries our team leader Chiang Chien-wei's article. It's titled "Only by Thorough Destruction Is It Possible to Build Firmly". Fine! I think the old things in our team have been destroyed all right, and the new built firmly enough!"

But when the people happily set up the date for the sale of summer grain to the state, in order to do more for the revolution, something unexpected happened.

It happened one day when a few commune members were transporting muddy rice for sale to the state. The comrades at the grain station found it and criticized them, and the muddy rice was turned back. But some members didn't accept the criticism, saying: "Rice grows out of the mud; naturally it's going to have a little mud on it!"

Quite a few people later blamed the transporters for delivering muddy rice to the state. The team leader, Chiang Chien-wei, was very upset. It was clearly wrong to sell muddy rice to the state; why should some people insist on doing so, not even listening to criticism? Chienwei recalled a previous event.

In 1969 the production team had tried to prevent capitalist tendencies by making regulations forbidding "free marketing", selling at high prices and other economic abuses, thinking that so long as the door was closed tight no evil wind could blow in. But there were some who had broken the regulations and sold collective produce at high prices, claiming they were "adding to the collective income". Through studying Chairman Mao's instruction: *There is no construction without destruction*, and repudiating "free marketing" and other capitalist tendencies, they came to realize that "destruction" and "construction" are a dialectical unity, that the former presupposes the latter. The same was true of trying to correct without repudiating; it was impossible, and nothing could be accomplished that way. As the masses' consciousness was raised, new regulations were established in people's minds, and these were translated into action. Once, when someone had wanted to sacrifice fuel in exchange for high-priced fish from the 8th team, the commune members turned down the deal.

Now, why had this muddy rice incident occurred? Chiang Chien-wei just couldn't imagine. What ought to be discarded had been discarded, what ought to be built up had been built. Why, then? Chiang Ju-wang came to discuss the question with him. They started by studying "*On Contradiction*" where Chairman Mao says: "*The unity of opposites is conditional, temporary and relative, while the struggle of mutually exclusive opposites is absolute.*" Ju-wang explained this to Chien-wei with deep feeling: "The struggle between socialism and capitalism is absolute. So while we've dug deep in one place it would be still shallow in other places; where we've built solidly there are still flaws." Chairman Mao's philosophic concept gave Chien-wei a better understanding of the relation between destruction and construction.

Yes, thorough destruction and firm construction are relative. Only repeated repudiation could constantly deepen the destruction and continuously strengthen the construction. Those who thought that one or two mass repudiation meetings were enough to thoroughly destroy the old and solidly construct the new, and that nothing more need be done, were thinking metaphysically and going against materialist dialectics as taught by Chairman Mao. Only by making revolutionary mass criticism every day, every year and always, is a socialist land guaranteed against changing color. The reason why muddy rice was going to the state was because revolutionary criticism had been relaxed. It reflected selfishness coming to the fore again.

When they saw through things, they had a way. That night the 8th team held a criticism meeting, and the commune members spoke one after another.

Wu Ai-chu, a woman member of the commune, said with emotion: "Most of us wanted to sell five hundred jin of clean rice to the state, but some disagreed, saying we should keep the clean rice for ourselves. Actually, what this amounted to was keeping our selfish ideas and personal considerations." Thus the discussion continued, and the people understood better what the socialist road was. They expressed their will to get rid of personal and departmental selfishness, and to sell their best grain to the state.

In high spirits early the next morning, they transported their best rice to the grain station, Chien-wei taking the lead. On the way, as he went over in his mind what had happened, he thought aloud: "Let a day pass without mass repudiation and you won't see through capitalism; let two days pass and you'll find yourself standing on the wrong side; go three days without criticizing what's wrong and you'll be a prisoner of revisionism. Relaxing criticism for longer than that puts the country in danger of changing color." An old poor peasant agreed:

"Criticizing capitalist evils is just like digging weeds from a field. After digging them out you have to rake them up, then hoe again and again so they won't take root again. Let's follow Chairman Mao all the way along the socialist road till we reach communism."

PHILOSOPHY IN IDEOLOGICAL EDUCATION

A Story of Homespun

A bride named Liu Ho-yu had married into Chinchien Production Brigade. She brought a hand loom with her, thinking: "In my new home, I may use this loom to weave homespun as a side cottage occupation. I'll have nice clothes to wear, pocket money to spend, and make use of my weaving ability."

At first Ho-yu was influenced by the commune members' enthusiasm to grasp revolution and promote production, often joining them in collective labor in the daytime and weaving only in her spare time or on rainy days. But gradually she was dulled and thought to herself that it was better to weave at home and earn money than get sunburned outside. She seldom joined in collective labor, and if she did occasionally attend the political study class she would sit at the back of the room thinking about weaving more homespun and paid no attention to discussion of revolutionary work and collective production.

Looking at the loom with envious eyes, Ho-yu's seventeen-year-old sister-in-law persuaded her father to make one for her. She learned how to weave from Hoyu, and then the two made homespun all day long, even forgetting to eat. Word of this spread quickly throughout the brigade, and many young women followed their example. The more the women wove, the less they joined in collective labour, and a small matter once out of hand soon developed into a big problem.

In order to correctly handle the relation between collective production and side cottage occupation, the brigade Party branch held a philosophy study class and called Ho-yu to join.

Party branch secretaries Chiang Ju-wang and Tai Hsiang-mei led the commune members in studying Chairman Mao's instructions on from quantitative to qualitative change. They spoke about what they had gained from the study. It is a tradition in the brigade that the Party cadres always spoke first in the study class.

Ju-wang pointed at a cup on the table and said: "Can this cup be filled with water?" The commune members answered: "Of course it can,"

Ju-wang continued: "Yes, this cup can be filled with water, even with a small crack at the top. But when we break it, bit by bit, and a quantitative change becomes qualitative, the cup becomes a pile of pieces and won't hold water. Our collective economy is also like the cup, if we make more cracks in it, it will collapse and capitalism will be restored. That is also from quantitative to qualitative change."

The commune members then understood what was meant by quantitative into qualitative change, and they discussed and criticized the capitalist thinking.

They said: "Capitalism is like sugar-coated arsenic. It may taste sweet today, but will destroy you tomorrow."

The enthusiastic discussion educated Ho-yu greatly.

After the study class Tai Hsiang-mei had a heart-to-heart talk with Ho-yu, saying sincerely:

"Ho-yu, it's not that side cottage occupation is not allowed, but it should be done in leisure time and not prevent the development of the collective economy. If we concentrate our energy on side occupation to the exclusion of collective labor, then 'side' becomes 'principal', and then it's wrong.

We should handle correctly the relation among state, collective and individual, and not forget the struggle between public and self. Once individualism takes hold, collectivism will suffer. You're anxious to earn money. You'll weave one metre of cloth the first day, and next day you'll want to weave more in order to earn more. By the third day you may think about getting rich. Soon you'll get mixed up and lose your bearings."

Ho-yu returned home, and the more she thought about what Hsiang-mei had said, the more she felt she was wrong. She asked herself: Am I going from quantitative to qualitative change? At first I was satisfied to earn a little pocket money by weaving, but once I see the money, I forget the struggle between the two lines. Capitalist ideas occupy my mind little by little, and make me sink deeper and deeper. Finally the quantitative change becomes qualitative, side occupation becomes principal, and I forget both collective production and class struggle but just sit at my loom. I weave and so does my sister-in-law, and other women commune members too. Such a development will certainly result in one's ideology becoming revisionist and revolutionary spirit being dampened, so that capitalism is finally restored. It's like fine rain soaking through one's clothes. How dangerous!

In the next study class Ho-yu talked about her study of the theory of quantitative into qualitative change and was praised by the commune members for applying the theory in practice. Later on Ho-yu helped other commune members to handle correctly the relation between collective production and side cottage occupation, raising higher their initiative in joining collective production.

Without Pebbles Big Stones Can Not Make a Wall

A complicated problem arose: How to handle the contradiction between stronger and weaker labor power in Chinchien Brigade?

One day when Secretary Chiang Ju-wang went to the 5th team, he overheard an argument between two men and two women who had been assigned to work the waterwheel that day.

The two men complained: "Just our bad luck to be assigned to work with two women; we have to do most of the work."

The women commune members protested: "You may be stronger and get higher wages, but in pedalling the wheel you exploit us."

"How do we exploit you?"

"All of us pedal the wheel with our feet, there's no difference. But your wages are higher than ours. Is this not exploitation?"

The two men were stumped and said: "Let's drop it. Anyhow a hen can't crow like a cock, and a woman is a woman."

Chiang was listening and thinking: "It sounds like a major contradiction. What's the nature of it? Which is the principal aspect? I must investigate and think over to find the principal aspect." Chiang decided to call a meeting and let the masses air their views.

That evening when the commune members gathered for the meeting Chiang started off: "Today strong workers had an argument with weaker ones. Let's talk about this problem tonight. There's a contradiction which should be exposed and analysed. The two aspects of the contradiction should present their views clearly. Both strong workers and the weaker ones should speak. Now, who will speak first?"

No sooner had he finished than a strong man jumped up and said, "The weaker ones pull us back. Women are not only weaker, they don't know how to work either. They're just a drag on us. If the whole team were strong workers, we could guarantee harvests increasing twenty or thirty per cent every year."

The team leader followed up: "That's right. The weaker ones are always dragged along by the stronger. Without strong workers for the ploughing and threshing there would be no crops."

The women members retorted angrily: "That's enough! You're strong, so of course everything you say about work goes. We of course have no right at all to speak."

This retort struck Chiang, and he felt that the principal aspect of the contradiction was the stronger labor power. Most of the team leaders and technicians in agricultural work are men who usually have the last say. He himself had in the past listened more to them, and this was one-sidedness on his part. He should also listen to those with weaker labour power so as to get a full picture of the problem. Then he raised the question: "Do strong workers remain strong workers under all circumstances? Is it not possible for them to become the weaker ones?"

The commune members were puzzled by this question. Chiang went on: "We must always remember this teaching of Chairman Mao: '*We must learn to look at problems all-sidedly, seeing the reverse as well as the obverse side of things.*' So we must listen not only to the strong workers but also to the weaker ones' opinions."

After a silence a young man spoke up. "I think the status of strong or weak is not absolute, but relative. Take me for example, this year I'm only seventeen so I'm not a strong worker. But in ten years I'll be twenty seven and I will be one, won't I?"

An old man added: "When I was young I was a strong worker, but now I'm sixty so I've become a weak one, haven't I?"

Everyone chuckled. A woman spoke next. "The team leader has said ploughing and threshing depend on strong workers. That's a one-sided way of looking at things. Without the buffalo boys to tend the buffalos, how would we plough? Without the women to dry the rice, could we eat it?"

A man answered: "That's right. If we tended the buffalos or sunned the rice, we wouldn't be making full use of our strength, would we?"

Another added: Women seem to be weaker workers, but in pig raising none of the strong workers can compare with them."

"It's like that in other work too," a woman rose and said. Pointing to a strapping young man of about twenty, she said: Last time we went to dig peanuts, you went for only two days and each day you only dug twenty *jin*. I went for five days and dug forty jin every day. And at the end of the second day you were standing up to stretch yourself and complain how tired you were. I see stars when I stand up!' you said, and you didn't show up any more."

Everybody laughed.

Secretary Chiang Ju-wang felt he could now sum up the discussion and said: "We can not look at things absolutely. Strong and weak are the two aspects of a contradiction, but each exists in the other and is related to the other."

"That's right. Without pebbles large stones can not make a wall," an old poor peasant said.

Chiang continued: 44 Under certain conditions strength can become weakness and vice versa. No matter what one's strength, if it is not commanded by proletarian politics, if he's not working for the revolution, he will have no drive or enthusiasm and even a strong person can become weak. If he has determination to farm for the revolution, to give all his ability and energy, even one who is weak can become strong.

Look at our brigade's Chiang Cheng-liang. He's nearly sixty. People may think of him as a weak worker. But since he criticized the wrong capitalist idea of using the hoe in two different ways for two different purposes, he has used his hoe exclusively for socialism and has even more drive than the young men. So are all people armed with Marxism Leninism-Mao Zedong Thought strong and militant. The most important thing is that once we are armed with Mao Zedong Thought we will have the communist style of work to contribute more for the collective economy as a glory, and not consider only ourselves."

Through the argument over weak and strong workers the commune members came to understand the law of the unity of opposites. The strong and weak workers have become more united and worked harder shoulder to shoulder to build the socialist countryside.

What's to Be Learned from Tachai*

In autumn 1968 Chiang Ju-wang visited Tachai and studied its experience, which has deeply influenced him in educating the peasants in Mao Zedong Thought and in the revolutionary spirit of conquering nature by hard struggle and self-reliance. Chiang Ju-wang determined to build Chinchien Brigade like Tachai.

On his return, he saw the slogans "Learn from Tachai" and "Learn Tachai's spirit, take Tachai's road" in the brigade and was very excited to see these signs of a vigorous mass movement to learn from Tachai.

That evening Chiang Ju-wang reported Tachai's experience to the poor and lower-middle peasants, and after

---

*Tachai, a production brigade of Hsiyang County, Shansi Province, is a standard-bearer in China's agriculture in building a socialist countryside with self-reliance and hard work. Chairman Mao in 1964 issued the great call: "*In agriculture, learn from Tachai.*"

The meeting more than eighty activists discussed how to learn from Tachai. A team leader stood up and said: "Let's start learning from Tachai immediately. I think we should take Tachai's business accounting system with the brigade as an accounting unit right now!" But the activists' opinion on this was divided, some nodding and some just keeping silent. Finally one young man said: "With the brigade as a business accounting unit, we shall have more labor power and more capacity. I think that's the way to build socialism."

One of the brigade leaders said: "We're always having conflicts among the production teams, say in irrigation problems. If we change our accounting unit from team to brigade, it will eliminate such conflicts and our work will be easier."

Someone else said: "We're not learning from Tachai if we don't take the production brigade as an accounting unit." Many commune members agreed. In fact, most of the activists favored taking a decision to make the brigade an accounting unit.

Chiang Ju-wang thought: This is an important matter. How can we decide it so quickly? Chiang remembered Chairman Mao's teaching: "*Investigation may be likened to the long months of pregnancy, and solving a problem to the day of birth. To investigate a problem is, indeed, to solve it.*" He decided to investigate further.

When Chiang went to the 2nd team many people surrounded him suggesting that it was better to make the change. The team leader pointed out many shortcomings with the production team as accounting unit, saying: "Our team is small, our land poor, and our income is low — all a result of the production team being an accounting unit. Only by making the change can we change our poor and bad condition."

Chiang then went to the 5th team where the commune members were enthusiastically discussing the question. But at his approach they stopped, and when he asked their opinion they said nothing. Then the team leader spoke up.

"As the majority of the brigade prefer the brigade accounting unit, of course we shall agree." Then hesitantly he asked: "How are we going to settle our financial problem?"

When Chiang went to the 9th team the team leader answered right out: "We have no preference whether it's brigade or team accounting unit."

Why did the three team leaders give three different answers? Chiang Ju-wang analyzed their comments and understood. There were three different conditions in the three teams: The 2nd team responded favorably to brigade accounting because its production level was low and the change was profitable for them. The 5th team, with its higher economic level and surplus funds of public accumulation did not agree with brigade accounting, but they would not voice opposition against it for fear that the other team members might criticize them as not favoring learning from Tachai. The 9th team's production was neither low nor high, so it made no difference to them what accounting unit was taken.

This investigation enlightened Chiang Ju-wang on the situation. At the brigade cadres' meeting, he said: "To learn from Tachai is to learn its fundamental experience, which is: to persist in putting proletarian politics in command and ideological leadership in the first place; to educate the commune members by conscientiously implementing the principles of self-reliance and hard work and the communist style of ardently loving the country and the collective." Chiang Ju-wang continued: "To learn from Tachai we must start from man's thinking and grasp firmly the struggles between the proletariat and the bourgeoisie, between the socialist and the capitalist roads, and between the revolutionary and the revisionist lines. Learning from Tachai depends upon which road we take, in which direction we go."

Chiang Ju-wang read a quotation from Chairman Mao's philosophic essay "*On the Correct Handling of Contradictions Among the People*": "*Socialist relations of production have been established and are in harmony with the growth of the productive forces, but they are still far from perfect, and this imperfection stands in contradiction to the growth of the productive forces.*"

Chiang and the other cadres analysed the specific situation in the brigade and arrived at the conclusion that three-level ownership of the means of production with the production team as basic unit* is in harmony with the growth of the productive forces; Chinchien Brigade was no exception. The important thing to learn from Tachai was not Tachai's brigade accounting unit but Tachai's political line.

When one of the cadres asked how they could settle the irrigation problems among the production teams without making the brigade the accounting unit, Chiang answered: "The productive forces of the people's commune are in harmony with the relations of production, but there are still some contradictions between them. As for using water from the reservoirs, sometimes there are conflicts among the production teams, but the problem can be solved mainly by political, ideological work and a reasonable arrangement." He continued: "Most of our brigade members do not understand the brigade accounting unit. Some teams prefer it in order to profit themselves, while others are afraid it will be unprofitable for them. If we change the accounting unit now from team to brigade, the problem of using reservoir water will not be solved, on the contrary, there will be new problems obstructing the growth of the productive forces."

---

*The economy of collective ownership in the rural people's commune at the present stage generally takes the form of three level ownership with the production team at the basic level, namely, ownership by the commune, the production brigade and the production team, with the production team as the basic accounting unit.

Another cadre disagreed, saying: "With the brigade accounting unit the cadres' work will be easier."

But Chiang did not think so. He said: "To take the brigade as the basic accounting unit is to strengthen collective economy and consolidate proletarian dictatorship. Just to think about making our work easier is selfishness and personal consideration. We must consider Party policy, not our own convenience."

"Are there any good points to be learned from Tachai's management?" a cadre asked.

"The over-all system of Tachai's administration and management represents the socialist direction, undertaken for consolidating the collective economy and persisting on the socialist road. According to our specific conditions we may follow some of Tachai's experience in administration and management. Not to do so would be one-sided."

Thus after lively discussion the cadres arrived at a clear understanding of what's to be learned from Tachai, and they decided that Chinchien Brigade should keep on the three-level ownership of the means of production with the team, not the brigade, as basic unit.

"The fundamental experience of Tachai from which we ought to learn is its persistence in educating, fostering and remolding the peasants in Mao Zedong Thought' said Chiang Ju-wang, summing up the discussion. "That's the socialist way. If we want only to learn the forms but not the principal experience, we'll go astray and finally lose even the forms we've learned."

Great changes have taken place in Chinchien Production Brigade since the commune members began their study of Chairman Mao's philosophic works several years ago. Their political and ideological consciousness has risen greatly, and their grain output exceeded 1,000 *jin* per *mu*.

The brigade is now an advanced unit in the study of philosophy, for which the brigade Party branch committee gives all credit to Chairman Mao and the Party. It recently carried out open-door rectification, encouraging the people to give their opinions and point out shortcomings, criticizing complacency and conservatism for preserving past glories.

Party branch committee members and peasants go to other advanced units to study their experience. They pledge to view achievements and honours correctly, from the angle of one dividing into two, and never to become conceited over achievements, but to find shortcomings when they are praised. They are determined always to follow Chairman Mao closely and continue the revolution.

Success out of failure. Chinchien Brigade used Chairman Mao's philosophic thinking, summed up experience, and planted tea shrubs on virgin hill slopes where peach and tung oil trees had not done well.